FIND YOUR TALENT

MAKE AN ANIMATION!

Sarah Levete

W

FRANKLIN WATTS
LONDON • SYDNEY

This paperback edition published in 2014

First published in 2012 by Franklin Watts

Franklin Watts
338 Euston Road
London NW1 3BH

Franklin Watts Australia
Level 17/207 Kent Street, Sydney NSW 2000

Produced by Arcturus Publishing Limited,
26/27 Bickels Yard, 151-153 Bermondsey Street, London SE1 3HA

Text: Sarah Levete
Editors: Joe Harris and Sarah Eason
Design: Paul Myerscough
Cover design: Akihiro Nakayama

Picture credits:
Cover images: Arcturus: Adam Clay bl, Jim Hansen ccr; iStockphoto: Artemis Gordon tl; Shutterstock: Yuri Arcurs ct, DM7 cl, Ioannis Ioannou tl, KUCO bc, Natalie-art br, Troyka tr, Tom Wang cr, OtnaYdur ccl.
Interior images: Arcturus: Adam Clay 4bl, 25tl, Darren McKee 7l, Q2E India 10cr; Corbis: Louie Psihoyos/ Science Faction 11b; Dreamstime: Colin Brothwood 15br, Maria Dryfhout 8bl, Kornilovdream 26-27tc, Maxim Shebeko 14tr; iStockphoto: Artemis Gordon 3b, 19cr, Marco Prandina 13t; Library of Congress: 9cl, 9cr, 18tr; Shutterstock: 29september 5bl, Alexnika 14bc, Animantz 22bl, Yuri Arcurs 29tr, Ellen Beijers 17bl, Nadezhda Bolotina 17cr, Michael D Brown 7b, Ant Clausen 24bl, Bairachnyi Dmitry 20cr, Lev Dolgachov 01, Envita 16br, Markus Gann 3c, 12tr, HitToon.com 18br, Lasse Kristensen 27cr, Jin Young Lee 20bl, Lineartestpilot 10tr, Dmitry Naumov 13bl, Giuseppe Parisi 28-29tc, Picsfive 27bl, Danilo Sanino 23bl, Pindyurin Vasily 21l, Chepko Danil Vitalevich 4bl, OtnaYdur 22-23tc; Wikipedia: Self 6bl.

A CIP catalogue record for this book is available from the British Library.

Dewey Decimal Classification Number 777.7-dc23

ISBN-13: 978 1 4451 3124 5

Printed in China

Franklin Watts is a division of Hachette Children's Books, an Hachette UK company.
www.hachette.co.uk

SL002140EN
Supplier 03 Date 1113 Print run 3061

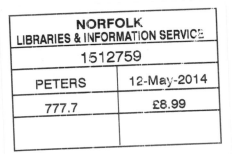

CONTENTS

FIND YOUR TALENT!

H ave you ever watched an animated film or TV programme and wondered how it was made? Have you ever thought about having a go? Well, now is the time to make a start. You will have fun and you may even discover you have a real talent.

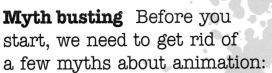

Trick of the eye!

So what is animation? Animate means 'bring to life' – the subject could be a picture, puppet or toy. In an animation, what you see is a series of still pictures. Each image is slightly different from the one before. It is the speed at which the pictures are shown that tricks the eyes into thinking that the pictures are moving.

Myth busting Before you start, we need to get rid of a few myths about animation:

- **You have to be a brilliant artist.** Wrong! You can animate simple stick figures or modelling clay faces. Of course, many animators are fantastic artists but it is not essential.
- **You need the most up-to-date camera and computer.** Wrong! A basic digital camera or scanner and a computer with some simple software will do.

Animation is all about tricking the eye into thinking that a still image is moving.

Most animators discover their talent for animation at home. For example, two of today's most successful animators began their careers at the kitchen table. Peter Lord and Dave Sproxton's first animation was a chalk figure on a blackboard. For each frame, the young hopefuls rubbed out a bit of the chalk, redrew it and shot it again. They then repeated the process again and again! Today, Peter Lord and his childhood friend run the hugely successful Aardman Animations, makers of films such as the hilarious *Chicken Run*.

Animating models made out of clay is called claymation.

Let's go! From drawings to action toys, you can bring anything to life. Well, not quite literally to life, but you get the picture! Over the next few pages, you will see just how easy animation can be.

MOVING PICTURES

Many animators start off by making flipbooks or flickbooks. These are 'books' made from a series of pictures or photographs that each change slightly. When you flip the pages, the pictures appear to move.

INSIDE STORY: SIMON'S CAT

Inspired by his favourite cartoons, British animator Simon Tofield began making flipbooks when he was very young. He uploaded his first animations onto the video-sharing website YouTube. The word spread and Simon's animations about his four cats received thousands of hits. Since then, *Simon's Cat* has been turned into books and a cartoon in a national newspaper.

Any sequence of movements, such as these old film images, can be joined together in a flipbook to create a moving picture.

Flipped out pictures The best way to start animating is by making your own flipbook out of a simple sequence or action. This sequence could be anything, such as a figure kicking a ball or a ball bouncing down some stairs. This will give you a sense of how pictures appear to move and how each frame in an animation needs to work.

GO FOR IT: FLIPPING MAGIC

Why not make your own flipbook? All you need are about 24 small sheets of paper (all the same size), a bulldog clip and a pencil or pen:

- Use the bulldog clip to fasten the sheets of paper together on one side. These will be your frames.
- Draw the first image in your sequence on the first sheet of paper. Keep the image towards the open edge of the pad so you will be able to see it when you flick the pages.
- Change the image slightly in each drawing – you will need about 24 frames for the effect of movement.
- Hold the bulldog clip, flip with your thumb and watch the action in motion. This is the start of your animation adventure!
- When you feel confident, you could try putting photographs of a model that you have moved in each frame onto the pages.

By studying the movements of people in real life, animators can recreate them in their characters.

Animate all the key stages in the movement of a subject, then watch it come to life!

THE BASICS

Y ou've seen how easy it is to create a moving picture with a flipbook. Now, it's time to get to grips with the basic process of animation.

Many animators start off by drawing their characters before moving onto other media.

GO FOR IT: STEP-BY-STEP

These are the key stages in making an animation:
- Brainstorm to find an idea for your animation.
- Choose your medium.
- Write a synopsis for your story.
- Make a storyboard. This is a cartoon strip that shows the key parts of the story.
- Start drawing, model-making or cutting out your images.
- Create a background or set for your characters.
- Photograph every different move you wish your character to make.
- Scan the images or upload them from a digital camera.
- Add any sound effects or speech.
- Finally, edit the animation.
- Watch, and be amazed!

Touchy feely One of your biggest questions will be whether to draw or use models. Doodle to see whether drawing is for you. Try experimenting with materials such as clay to see if you prefer animating models. Play around with bringing an action toy to life or cut out some paper puppets. For your animation, use whichever medium you enjoy the most.

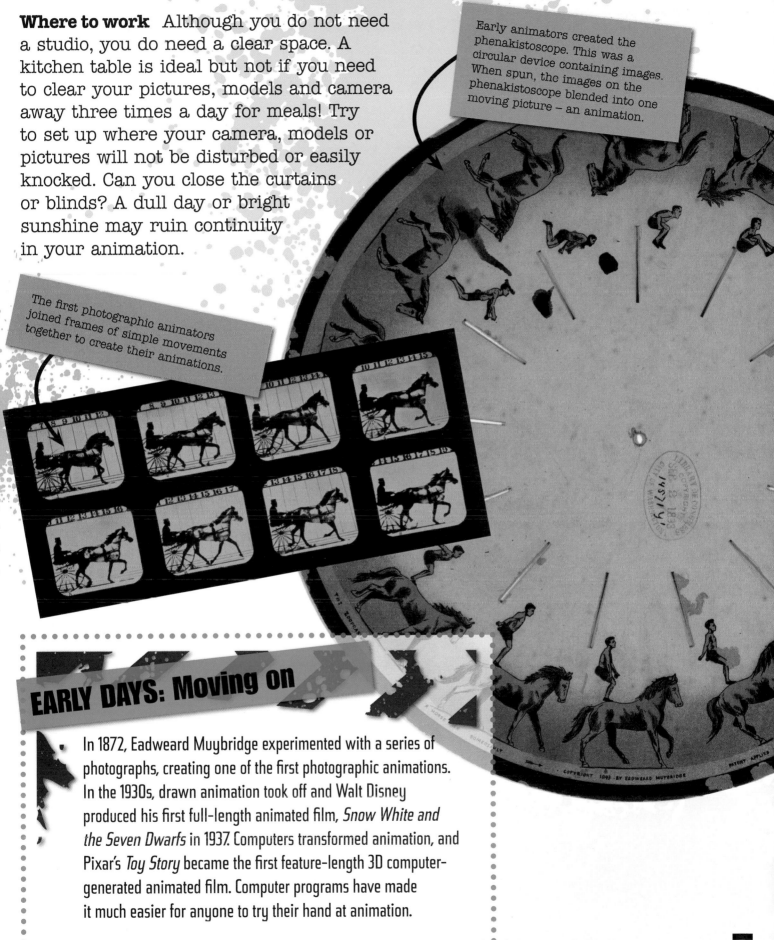

Where to work Although you do not need a studio, you do need a clear space. A kitchen table is ideal but not if you need to clear your pictures, models and camera away three times a day for meals! Try to set up where your camera, models or pictures will not be disturbed or easily knocked. Can you close the curtains or blinds? A dull day or bright sunshine may ruin continuity in your animation.

Early animators created the phenakistoscope. This was a circular device containing images. When spun, the images on the phenakistoscope blended into one moving picture – an animation.

The first photographic animators joined frames of simple movements together to create their animations.

EARLY DAYS: Moving on

In 1872, Eadweard Muybridge experimented with a series of photographs, creating one of the first photographic animations. In the 1930s, drawn animation took off and Walt Disney produced his first full-length animated film, *Snow White and the Seven Dwarfs* in 1937. Computers transformed animation, and Pixar's *Toy Story* became the first feature-length 3D computer-generated animated film. Computer programs have made it much easier for anyone to try their hand at animation.

CLASSICAL STYLE

Let's look at some different types of animation that you could try. Once you've decided which one works for you, you can start to plan your cartoon. First, let's look at classical drawn animation.

Some of the simplest drawn animations are the most effective. You can choose to work either in black and white or in colour.

GO FOR IT: START YOUR ART

To start a hand-drawn animation, you will need this equipment:

- A hole punch makes holes at the edge of each piece of paper.
- A peg bar keeps the paper in position for each new drawing. It is a bar with two pegs fixed to it. The pegs go through the punched holes in the paper. If you cannot find a peg bar in your local art shop, you can make your own one. Ask an adult to help you fix two pegs to a wooden ruler.
- A light box lets you see several drawings at once, so that you can easily trace them. You can make your own light box by shining a light under a piece of perspex.

Keep it simple Every line in drawn animation needs to be redrawn for each frame, so make life easy! Instead of lots of hair, stick to a few curls. Avoid detail such as logos or numbers on clothes – you will come to hate them if you need to draw them over 12 times for just one second of action! Don't forget to number your pictures.

Time cheat Once you have a feel for drawn animation and want to save time, use cels (transparent sheets of film). First, draw the background onto some paper. Next, draw anything that changes position on the cels. Then, place the cels onto the background.

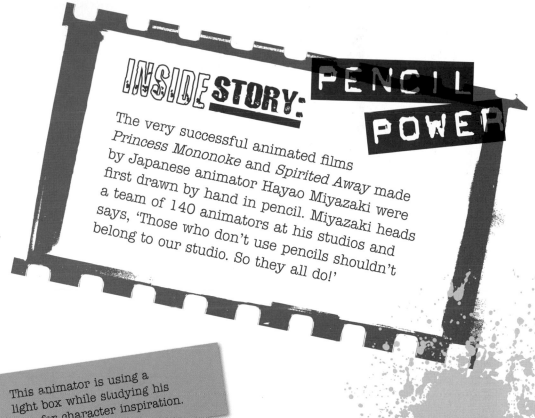

INSIDE STORY: PENCIL POWER

The very successful animated films *Princess Mononoke* and *Spirited Away* made by Japanese animator Hayao Miyazaki were first drawn by hand in pencil. Miyazaki heads a team of 140 animators at his studios and says, 'Those who don't use pencils shouldn't belong to our studio. So they all do!'

This animator is using a light box while studying his face for character inspiration.

JUNK YARD

I f you don't want to draw, try animating objects found around your house. You can use anything from toys, such as old action figures, dolls or building blocks, to fruit, vegetables and even junk.

Think outside the box Look around your house for old cardboard boxes. By joining together boxes of different sizes you can create a fun character.

Raid the toy box Your old toys are just waiting to be brought to life again! Take a look at cars, balls, toy trains and other discarded toys. Make sure that the toys can stand up on their own or will stay put with sticky tack.

Animate a figure made from cardboard boxes. Check the limbs stay in position when you move them.

GO FOR IT: TALKING FRUIT AND VEG

It's time to make your fruit talk!:
- Find some fruit or vegetables, such as apples, potatoes or bananas.
- Use a pen to draw in different expressions on the fruit and vegetables.
- Push pipe cleaners or bendy straws into the fruit and vegetables to make arms and legs.

A Lego car and characters can be used to create a fantastic animation.

Talking toys If you choose toys or models that have moveable parts, check that you can move them easily. You can find some amazing examples of animated Lego toys on YouTube. These animations even have their own name – brickfilms.

INSIDE STORY: LEGEND ON FILM

In 2003, a full-length animation called *The Legend of the Sky Kingdom* made it into the top five at the International Animated Film Festival in France. The Zimbabwean film-makers made their models out of junk, such as scrapped car parts, because that was all they could afford. 'The idea of making a movie out of nothing really appealed to me, and I think it fired our creativity and passion in a way that proved you don't need big money and experience – what matters is passion and determination,' said director Roger Hawkin.

It's easy to add character and expression to a simple apple.

MAKE YOUR OWN

You can be super creative and make your own models to animate. You do not need elaborate puppets or expensive clays. Instead, use any material – as long as it is flexible and can be moved several times without breaking.

Knitted up Young animator Charlotte Blacker's prize-winning animation called *The Little Red Plane* featured models made from wool. What are you waiting for? Start knitting!

Look for modelling materials in toy or craft shops, which you can use to create your characters.

Woollen characters should be made with a wire 'skeleton' inside to support their shape and to make the character's arms and legs moveable for animation shots.

Get bendy Modelling clay is great for moulding, but it weakens when it gets hot. Take care not to shine bright lights onto it! Bend, twist, push, press and squash the clay to shape it. Experiment with the feel and shape. For extra support, you could make a frame or skeleton before adding the moulding material – bendy wire, foil or pipe cleaners can all be twisted into a basic shape.

GO FOR IT: READY TO ROLL

Follow these basic tips to make sure your model is shoot-fit:
- Keep the design bold and simple. A fussy design is harder to move or reproduce if it breaks.
- Make sure the model can stand up on its own.
- Check you can move the body parts easily and the arms do not break off every time you change the pose.
- Take care that you don't leave dirty fingerprints on soft materials such as modelling clay.

If you don't like working with clay, you can create fabulous animation characters from plasticine instead.

INSIDE STORY: ALL CHANGE

Clay characters can be manipulated to change shape – and so character – dramatically. The Italian animators at Misseri Studio are famous for changing, or morphing, their clay cat characters from the children's TV animation show Mio Mao. The cats can turn into balls, leaves and even other animals! Take a look at them in action by typing 'Mio Mao' into www.youtube.com.

CUT IT OUT

Cut-out animation uses flat puppets made from paper, photos, or materials such as fuzzy felt. This kind of animation does not create smooth movements but it has a charming style.

Can you cut it? A simple shape can be cut out from coloured or patterned paper, or you can draw a more detailed character onto a sheet of blank paper, then cut it out.

Move it! Unlike classically sketched characters, cut-outs only need to be drawn once. This means you can make your character more detailed than a traditional drawn animation. Once you have created your character, cut it into moveable parts: legs, feet, head and body.

You can make your cut-out characters from cardboard.

GO FOR IT: THE BEST BITS

Get the best from your cut-out:
- Join it by sewing the parts together with a needle and thread. You can also use sticky tape to join the parts together.
- Use tweezers to move only the part of the cut-out that you want to move, without moving the whole character.
- To give a character a range of expressions, have several head cut-outs with different expressions or have separate eyebrows, eyeballs and mouths that you can add to your cut-out.
- Cover your cut-out with sticky-backed plastic to make it last longer. Check that the pieces still move.

In the background For a dramatic, stark look, choose a dark piece of paper for your background. If you go for a funky, patterned background, make sure it does not dominate your cut-outs. If you add in props such as toys or models, check they are in proportion to your cut-outs.

MIX AND MATCH

INSIDE STORY:

Cut-outs often suit the style of children's books. The TV cartoon *Charlie and Lola* (based on Lauren Child's books about a brother and sister) blends cut-outs, drawings and fabrics – the books are a mixture of painting, drawing and collage.

Old fabric can make a fantastic cut-out material.

Don't throw away wrapping paper – keep it to create cut-outs!

STORY TIME

N ow that you have chosen your medium, it is time to put your ideas onto paper. A storyboard will help you work out how your great idea is going to work as an animation.

Is your animation going to be a funny take on a tale or will you give it a more serious treatment?

Find your story If you want to develop a story, it is usually easier to start with something that you know well. You could also choose a scene from a classic fairy tale but give it your own spin. Sometimes, the most unlikely subject matter works – look at the huge success of Bart Simpson's bickering family! Look for inspiration wherever you are. Keep a notebook and pen with you so you can jot down any ideas.

Follow these simple steps to draw a complete storyboard:

- Draw some black frames on paper with space underneath where you can write a summary of the action or any details you want to include once you have your story.
- Break down your tale into a series of images that represent the actions taking place in the story.
- Draw these images roughly onto your storyboard frames.
- Write a simple paragraph that explains what is happening in the boxes below each frame.
- Add in any dialogue or details of other effects (such as sound) that could add to your story and its interest for the viewer.
- Note down how you will film each frame – do you want close-ups, long shots or do you need to see your character from the side?

Magic moments A storyboard is like a cartoon strip of the main moments in your animation. Working on it will help you to think about who is telling the story and what you want to show. It is a rough sketch so you do not have to spend time working up each drawing fully. Even if your animation is simple, storyboard it – otherwise you will not know which stages you need to shoot.

Working through a storyboard with a friend can throw up some great new ideas.

EARLY DAYS: Two years of storytelling

- Nick Park first developed the concept of the feature-length film *Wallace and Gromit: The Curse of the Were-Rabbit* by writing and drawing ideas with colleague Steve Box. It then took a lengthy two years to storyboard the idea – but it was well worth it!

To get a feel for the process of animation, film a very simple sequence of movements, such as a hand making a fist then opening out again. Look at the camera's manual to find out how you can film a single frame at a time. Use a camcorder, digital camera or smart phone.

GO FOR IT: STEADY

A camera that wobbles will not work for animation. To avoid wobble:

- Place the camera in front of the model and make sure it is steady.
- Set up a stand or tripod if you have one to keep the camera in place. If you do not have a tripod, set the camera on a pile of books and use some tape to keep it in place.
- For drawings or cut-outs (see pages 10–11 and 16–17), fix the camera above the images.

A tripod holds the camera steady.

Stop and move a model again and again to make it look as if it is moving. This is known as stop-motion animation.

Freebies You can use software that comes free with your computer, such as iMovie and Windows Movie Maker, to import your photos and run them as a film. To learn to use the programs, watch a tutorial online. You will be able to edit your animation, deleting frames or adding in extra ones by copying and pasting.

Look at your work to see if you need to add or rework any parts.

GO FOR IT: ALL IN THE ANGLE

To get the most out of filming, experiment with these angles and shot types:

- close-up – use this to emphasise a particular thing in a scene
- cut – a quick change where the shot is suddenly moved to another view
- cross-cut – cut from one action to another to make them look as if they are happening at the same time
- fade – let the image slowly fade from the screen
- long shot – show everything in the scene to give an overview of the character in the setting
- mid-shot – use to focus on the character's actions and words
- pan – let the camera move to a different part of a scene

Angle for effect You can use the camera angle to add atmosphere, mood and to enhance characterisation. If a character walks into a wall in your film, let the camera wobble! If you want to draw attention to a particular point in your animation, use a close-up angle and hold the shot for a second or two for impact.

Different points of view can make your animation more dynamic. A close-up shot can focus on facial expression. A full-body shot can show your character in action.

COMPUTER MAGIC

You can use a computer to both create the frames for your animation and then edit it. If you want to have a go at computer animation, search the internet for free programs and follow their tutorials.

3D computer animation Some of the major animation successes have been created by computers in three dimensions, or 3D. The animator designs the character but the computer creates the models. Characters are manipulated with the use of complex computer tools. If you want to explore 3D computer animation, you will need a powerful computer and a 3D animation package.

Before you download a program, check it is compatible with your computer system.

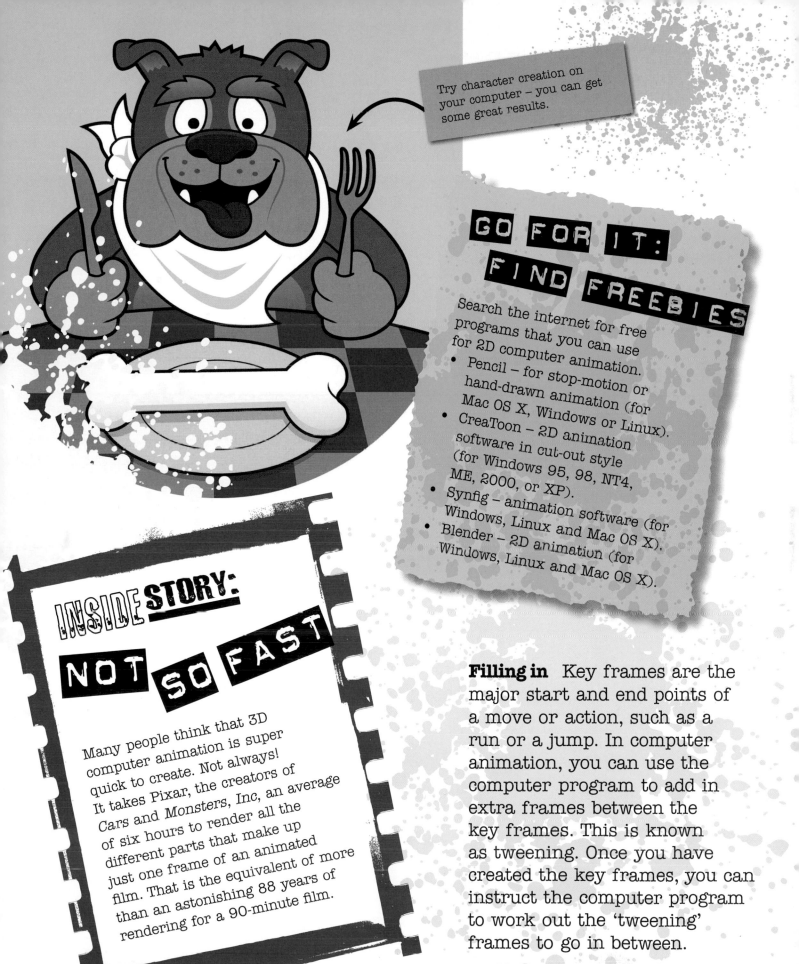

Try character creation on your computer – you can get some great results.

GO FOR IT: FIND FREEBIES

Search the internet for free programs that you can use for 2D computer animation.

- Pencil – for stop-motion or hand-drawn animation (for Mac OS X, Windows or Linux).
- CreaToon – 2D animation software in cut-out style (for Windows 95, 98, NT4, ME, 2000, or XP).
- Synfig – animation software (for Windows, Linux and Mac OS X).
- Blender – 2D animation (for Windows, Linux and Mac OS X).

INSIDE STORY: NOT SO FAST

Many people think that 3D computer animation is super quick to create. Not always! It takes Pixar, the creators of Cars and Monsters, Inc, an average of six hours to render all the different parts that make up just one frame of an animated film. That is the equivalent of more than an astonishing 88 years of rendering for a 90-minute film.

Filling in Key frames are the major start and end points of a move or action, such as a run or a jump. In computer animation, you can use the computer program to add in extra frames between the key frames. This is known as tweening. Once you have created the key frames, you can instruct the computer program to work out the 'tweening' frames to go in between.

SOUND IT OUT

Some brilliant animations have no sound at all. Others are transformed by the addition of sound effects or music – and the soundtrack helps the audience to connect with the animation. Search the internet for free audio downloads or record your own.

Voiceovers If you are giving your characters a voice, it is best to record it before you film. However, you then need to shoot your animation to fit the voice. If you want your character to look as if it is talking, draw the different shapes a person's mouth makes when saying different sounds so that you have some ready reference.

INSIDE STORY: WHO'S SPEAKING?

Who can forget Eddie Murphy's voice for the donkey in *Shrek* or Angelina Jolie voicing the Tigress in *Kung Fu Panda*? But when a team first sell their idea for a film, they record the dialogue. Sometimes, they are so good that they actually become the voice of the character for the final film!

Call on your friends to voice your characters and don't be shy about giving some direction!

GO FOR IT: MAKE SOME NOISE!

All you need is a microphone, imagination and to follow these steps to get the soundtrack right:

- If your computer doesn't have a built-in microphone, you will need to buy or borrow one.
- Search the internet for free recording and editing programs such as Audacity.
- Think outside the box — if you want to hear the sound of crackling flames, do not start a fire! Instead, scrunch up a crisp packet. Spin some bicycle wheels for wind and hit a table with a rolled up newspaper for a resounding 'thwack'!

Sound effects Add music and other sound effects when you have completed your animation. Until you can see your work, you will not know what the sound 'looks like'. For example, the sound of something breaking may need a heavy thud or a splintering, tinkling noise.

You can record simple sounds, such as a doorbell, to use in your animation film.

Scrunch up some paper – can you hear that it sounds like feet walking on gravel?

Copyright If you decide to use pre-recorded music you need to make sure you are legally allowed to do so. Recorded music is copyrighted. Contact the person or company that owns the licence and ask for permission to use it. You may have to pay a fee but it is important to make sure you stay within the law.

STEP UP A GEAR

Now that you have experimented with different animation media and you have made a couple of films, it is time to take your animation to the next level!

Show time! One of the easiest ways to reach a wide audience is through video-sharing websites such as YouTube, Metacafe and Dailymotion. You can decide if you want your animation available to anyone and everyone, or if you want to limit it to a select few of your friends. Read the small print though to see who will own the copyright once it is uploaded.

Screen it Arrange a screening for your friends and family. Ask for feedback. Do not take criticism personally! Rather, use their comments to help you to understand what other people like about your animation, and how you can improve it.

Courses There are plenty of classes or workshops you can take to develop your animation skills. Life drawing will help you to draw and create convincing figures with flowing movements. Writing classes will help you to structure and plan your story, and write the script.

Moving along Find out if there is a local animation group or training centre near you. Take some courses and then offer to help out. There are often competitions and festivals to enter. An internet search should help you access the relevant ones.

Make a portfolio If you are really serious about working in animation, you need a show reel or portfolio of your work. Include only the pieces that show your best work, not everything you have ever done. Before you send it to a company, do your research. Lots of companies do not accept unsolicited portfolios. If the company accepts show reels, try to find the name of the person to address it to so you can follow it up with them afterwards.

The future Animation is not just about the art of drawing or making a model move. There are so many elements to it. Think about which aspect you enjoy most and which you are best at. Animation companies can have huge teams working on one project, and any one of these roles might suit you:
• director
• storyboard artist
• camera operator
• moving model animator
• key drawing animator (showing the key moves)
• model-maker
• studio animator
• computer game animator

GLOSSARY

brainstorm to think of lots of ideas

brickfilms the name given to animations using brick toys such as Lego

cels short for celluloid: the transparent sheets on which animation drawings are traced and painted

claymation characters made from clay, such as Wallace and Gromit

collage using pieces of material or paper to make a picture

compatible works with

continuity consistency of appearance, even when something is filmed on different days

copyrighted when a piece of work is owned by an artist or musician. The owner has the right to refuse or give permission for others to use the work

customise to give an individual look to something

cut-outs flat animation figures cut from paper or other material with moveable parts, such as arms or legs

dialogue talking

director the person who has overall control of a project and decides what happens in the filming

edit to cut and move around to improve the overall animation

elaborate complicated

emphasise to draw attention to

fabric material

flexible to be able to move easily

frame a single image in a series of images that move quickly to create the illusion of movement

key frame the start and end point of a move

licence permission to use something

manipulated made to move

medium the material you use for animating

model sheet a sheet on which animators record details about each character, from size to look

peg bar a device that holds sheets of paper in position

perspex a see-through, tough plastic

portfolio a collection of your work

proportion to scale

props objects, such as furniture, used in a film or animation

render to turn computer data into visual images

resounding strong, noisy

sequence actions that take place in order

set the props and background used in an animation

show reel your best work presented on film or video

soundtrack a recording to go with a film

stop-motion animation using models

storyboard a cartoon strip that plots the key parts of an animation

surreal fantastical or dream-like

synopsis a summary of a story

three dimensional, or 3D an image that has height, width and gives the impression of depth

tripod a three-legged stand used to hold a camera steady

tweening when computer software creates the frames inbetween key frames

two dimensional, or 2D an image that has height and width

unsolicited not asked for

upload to transfer data onto a computer

FURTHER INFORMATION

Books

Cartoons and Animations by Richard Spilsbury (Heinemann, 2007)

Cracking Animation by Peter Lord and Brian Sibley (Thames and Hudson, 2010)

Learn to Draw Animated Cartoons by Janet Nunn (Collins, 2006)

Websites

You can search the internet for online tutorials on ways to animate models or building blocks.

Brickfilms

This website show some inventive uses of brick toys in animation:

**http://chrislegoproductions.webs.com/
   apps/videos/**

If you want some tips on making brickfilms, check out:

**www.zootproductions.com/
   FAQ.html
www.youtube.com/watch?v=6mEeQ4hO-8c**

Most of the big animation companies have useful websites:

DreamWorks

Check out this legendary animation company's incredible website:
www.dreamworksanimation.com

Pixar

Find out more about the makers of animation greats such as *Toy Story*:
www.pixar.com

INDEX